CW01431833

Original title:
Gnarled Hinges Under the Mermaid Carb

Author: Olivia Oja
ISBN HARDBACK: 978-1-80562-807-1
ISBN PAPERBACK: 978-1-80564-328-9

Timeless Groans of the Tidal Wave

In shadows deep where secrets dwell,
The ocean whispers, casting spells.
Beneath the moon's soft silver glow,
The tides conspire, begin to grow.

With each swell, the sand runs scared,
As distant dreams are softly shared.
The waves, they chant a sorrowed song,
Of timeless groans where hearts belong.

A ship adrift on darkened foam,
In haunted depths, it searches home.
The stars above, a twinkling crowd,
Bear witness to the lost, the loud.

Yet from the depths, a light will rise,
A beacon seen through stormy skies.
Embrace the surge, the pull, the push,
For from the dark, we find our hush.

So heed the waves, both fierce and meek,
In whispered tales, their truths will speak.
For in each crash, each soft caress,
Lies nature's song, a timeless bless.

Forgotten Songs of the Sea

In depths where silence weaves a tale,
Ghostly whispers ride the gale.
Shells adorned with stories old,
Murmured secrets, brave and bold.

Waves embrace the moon's soft glow,
Carving paths where few dare go.
Lighthouse beams, a guiding hand,
Cradling dreams on shifting sand.

Oceans cradle hearts once lost,
Each tide a memory, each wave a cost.
Songs of mariners lost at sea,
Echoing through eternity.

Seagulls call with voices clear,
A melody both sweet and dear.
Their cries entwined with the spray,
Charting tales of yesterday.

In the quiet of twilight's gleam,
Salt and sorrow form a dream.
The horizon beckons with a sigh,
As forgotten songs of the sea float by.

Cracks in the Fabric of Time

Through realms where shadows softly creep,
Time's own secrets whisper deep.
Cracks appear in the woven thread,
A tapestry of dreams long dead.

Each heartbeat echoes, soft yet loud,
Futures dance beneath the shroud.
Moments flicker, blink, and fade,
In the silence, memories laid.

Waves of time, relentless flow,
Carrying whispers only they know.
Fragments of laughter, tears unshed,
In the margins where silence spread.

Heroes lost in pages worn,
In every breath, a tale is born.
Cracks reveal a story's plight,
Lost and found in fading light.

Fleeting dreams like shadows play,
In the depths where echoes sway.
Through the rift, a truth unfolds,
In the cracks, the past retolds.

Chasing Echoes Underwater

Beneath the waves, where visions swirl,
Echoes chase in a silent whirl.
Fins glimmer under soft blue light,
Dancing shadows, shadows bright.

The ocean's heart beats deep and slow,
Carrying tales from long ago.
Bubbles rise with whispers of lore,
Secrets lurking on the ocean floor.

With every stroke, the currents guide,
Through realms where creatures gently hide.
Chasing echoes, lost in trance,
In fluid realms, we weave and dance.

The call of sirens sings to me,
In melodies of the ageless sea.
Ripples ripple, time does bend,
In the depths, the journey never ends.

As starlight fades into the dusk,
Waves whisper promises, soft and husk.
Chasing echoes, we entwine,
In ocean's embrace, our hearts align.

Castaways in a Sea of Memories

Upon the shore of faded dreams,
We gather fragments, silent beams.
Castaways on sands of time,
Collecting moments, weak and sublime.

The tide washes hearts of yore,
Echoing tales upon the shore.
Every whisper, a thread to weave,
In the tapestry that we believe.

Seashells cradle the past so dear,
Each a wish, a laugh, a tear.
Lost in echoes, we drift and sway,
In the currents, come what may.

Beneath the stars, our spirits roam,
In a sea of memories, we find home.
With every wave, we come alive,
In the ebb and flow, we will thrive.

So take my hand, let us explore,
Castaways on a never-ending shore.
In every heartbeat, truth we find,
In this vast sea, hearts intertwined.

Driftwood Diaries and Secrets

In shadows cast by ancient trees,
Whispers of driftwood ride the breeze.
Each splinter tells a tale untold,
Of distant shores and hearts of gold.

Beneath the waves, the stories sleep,
Nature's secrets buried deep.
Silent witnesses to the past,
In their embrace, memories last.

With every tide, they shift and sway,
Echoing dreams of yesterday.
Fragments of journeys carved by time,
In whispered verses, they softly chime.

So gather 'round, let's share the lore,
Of driftwood whispers from the shore.
In every grain, a world expands,
In secrets held by salty sands.

The Resilient Armor of Nature

Beneath the storm, the forest stands,
With roots that grip the ancient lands.
A shield of green against the skies,
Through rain and gale, it never cries.

The mountains rise, a timeless grace,
Their sturdy peaks a warm embrace.
Through crack and crevice, life will bloom,
Resilient hearts, dispelling gloom.

In every leaf, a tale unfolds,
Of battles fought, of truths retold.
A symphony of strength and peace,
In nature's arms, our doubts release.

So stand we tall, like trees so grand,
With hearts like rivers, strong and planned.
Together we will brave the night,
In nature's armor, find the light.

A Tale of Mesmerizing Tides

The ocean breathes a rhythmic song,
A melody where dreams belong.
Each wave a dancer in the light,
With secrets hidden out of sight.

The moon, a keeper of the flow,
Guides the tides with a gentle glow.
A tale unfolds with every crest,
An endless journey, never rest.

From sandy shores to depths unknown,
The tides weave stories all their own.
Whispers of sailors brave and true,
Carried on waves that kiss the blue.

So listen close, and you shall find,
The echoes of the sea, entwined.
In mesmerizing tides, we sail,
As dreams take wing, we shall not fail.

Lost Amongst the Waves

In salty sea, where dreams collide,
I drift away on a rising tide.
Each swell a promise, every spray,
A chance to find my lost ballet.

The horizon calls with whispers sweet,
While gentle currents guide my feet.
In depths unknown, I let them lead,
To find the peace my heart does need.

Amongst the waves, I lose my care,
To dance with echoes in the air.
The sun dips low, painting the skies,
As twilight weaves a tale of sighs.

So take my hand, let's drift away,
Where moonlit paths and starlight play.
In wanderlust, our spirits rise,
Lost amongst waves, we touch the skies.

Dance of Tide and Timeworn Metal

Beneath the moon's soft glow, they twirl,
Shadows sketching secrets in the swirl.
Waves play a melody, ancient and grand,
While the stars flicker gently, hand in hand.

Rusty chains whisper of sailors' tales,
Worn by the sea's caress and gales.
Each ripple tells stories of battles fought,
In the dance of tide, dreams are caught.

Once proud ships now lie in repose,
Overgrown with seaweed, nature's clothes.
But in their silent slumber, a call remains,
Echoing softly through time's vast lanes.

Here the past and present entwine tight,
As shadows and whispers drift into night.
Through every rise and fall of the tide,
The heart of the ocean beats with pride.

So waltz with the waves, let your spirit roam,
Find solace in history, call it home.
For in every ebb, there's a chance to see,
The dance of tide, entwined with destiny.

Coral Dreams and Iron Songs

Below the surface, a world unseen,
Where coral castles rise in shades of green.
Fish weave through gardens of vibrant light,
Painting dreams under the tranquil night.

Iron bells toll from wrecks long past,
A symphony written in shadows cast.
Echoes linger in the salt-laden air,
As memories drift like whispers, rare.

The deep holds secrets in its grasp,
While time slips by, a gentle clasp.
A dance of colors beneath the foam,
In this watery realm, the heart finds home.

With every tide, a new tale is spun,
Of sunken treasures and battles won.
Coral reefs sing in harmonies bold,
Iron songs of yore in stories told.

So dive deep into this sacred sea,
Let go of your worries, just be free.
For in these waters, dreams take flight,
As coral dances in the pale moonlight.

Beneath the Waves, a Hidden Door

Deep in the ocean's gentle lap,
Lies a door where the sea-spirits nap.
It's wrought from shells and driftwood fine,
Guarded by fish in a grand design.

With a hesitant touch, the door swings wide,
Revealing wonders the world can't bide.
Timeless beauty in every hue,
Where magic weaves its stories anew.

Beyond the door, the currents play,
Whispering secrets of yesterday.
Each wave that crashes, a soft embrace,
Inviting you into a hidden place.

Here, dreams are cradled by the tide,
In the heart of the ocean, time can't hide.
So linger awhile, let your spirit soar,
For beneath the waves lies the hidden door.

Step gently forth, let your heart decide,
To journey where waves and wonders hide.
In this vast blue, where stories convene,
Together we'll find what has always been.

Where Anchors Rust and Stories Begin

On shores where anchors lay in rust,
And dreams mix with the sea's soft trust.
Old vessels whisper tales of old,
The warmth of their stories a wonder to behold.

Salted winds carry echoes near,
Of sailors' songs and laughter clear.
Beneath the sand, a treasure chest lies,
Waiting for seekers with curious eyes.

The gulls circle high with knowing grace,
Guiding adventurers to this sacred space.
Where the past intertwines with lines of fate,
And every heartbeat flourishes, innate.

Here, time flows gently, like streams of light,
Illuminating the dark of night.
In the spaces where the heart can mend,
Is where the anchors rust and stories begin.

So sit by the shore, let the waves caress,
Each whisper, a promise, a sweet caress.
For in the rust of anchors, we shall find,
The tales of the ocean, forever entwined.

Surreal Reflections Along the Coast

Waves whisper tales of forgotten dreams,
Mirrored in the sands, where magic gleams.
Footprints of time, drifted and swirled,
A realm where sea magic unfurls.

Seagulls dance, wings wide and free,
Painting shadows against the sea.
The horizon blurs, a canvas untamed,
Where every heartbeat is softly named.

Twilight descends, cloaked in delight,
Stars awaken in the embrace of night.
The moon's soft glow, a silvery beam,
Guides the lost souls through worlds that teem.

Shells hold secrets of travelers past,
Whispers of wishes, dreams cast.
Each tide that recedes, a promise untold,
Of stories woven in currents of gold.

In this surreal realm, time drifts slow,
A tide of thoughts, like melodies flow.
Along the coast, where wonders reside,
Reflections shimmer with the ocean's pride.

Bridges in the Abyss

In shadows deep where echoes lie,
Bridges beckon 'neath the sky.
Gossamer threads weave through the dark,
Guiding the lost, igniting a spark.

Each step is laced with trials and fears,
The heart beats softly, tuned to the years.
With each bridge crossed, a tale unfolds,
Of heroes forged through brave, bold holds.

Beneath the surface, secrets entwined,
Mysteries wait for the daring mind.
Lost souls wander, searching for light,
In the abyss where darkness takes flight.

A shimmering path of silver and stone,
Promises whispers of safe return home.
With courage drawn from the depths of despair,
Life's fragile beauty hangs in the air.

As dawn breaks open, the abyss retreats,
New worlds emerge in the heart's soft beats.
Bridges may tremble, yet still hold fast,
Uniting the present with shadows of past.

Unveiling the Depths of Secrets

In whispered tones, the night reveals,
Layers of truth that time conceals.
A tapestry woven with shadows and light,
Secrets emerge from the depths of night.

Each glance is a portal, each sigh a key,
Unlocking worlds yet to be.
Beneath the surface, the heart knows best,
An odyssey waiting, a hidden quest.

Through corridors dim, where echoes play,
Fragments of stories hold sway.
Time dances softly, a fleeting sight,
Lifting the veil, revealing the light.

In corners dark, where memories hide,
The sea of secrets, endless and wide.
Fingers trace paths of those who dared,
To peer into wonders that love has shared.

With each revelation, shadows recede,
Forbidden whispers fulfill the need.
A journey embarked upon ancient tides,
Unveiling the depths where truth abides.

The Hidden Garden of Timeless Time

In quiet corners where shadows nest,
Lies a garden of dreams, softly blessed.
Whispers of blooms in colors aglow,
Time stands still in the magic below.

With petals that shimmer in morning light,
Each blossom cradles the secrets of night.
Vines intertwine, a tapestry bright,
In this sacred space, worries take flight.

The breeze carries songs of ages past,
While gentle hands weave dreams that last.
Under a canopy of shimmering stars,
Pain and joy bloom in hidden jars.

Footsteps tread softly on fragrant paths,
Around each corner, a new mystery laughs.
Memories linger in this haven serene,
In the garden, time is forever green.

So linger awhile in this cherished domain,
Where laughter and sorrow entwine like a chain.
In gardens hidden from the ticking chime,
Eternity breathes in the heart of time.

Moonlight on Weathered Wood

Beneath the silver glow of night,
The whispers play on beams of light.
Each shadow dances, softly sways,
In dreams of ancient, bygone days.

The weathered wood, with tales to tell,
For every ring, a magic spell.
A history carved from time so deep,
Where secrets of the forest sleep.

When moonlit beams adorn the floor,
They cast enchantments evermore.
In quietude, the world stands still,
Awaiting the heart's gentle thrill.

And every knot, a story spun,
Where shadows dance and laughter's fun.
For in this magic, hope ignites,
Through moonlit dreams on endless nights.

Twilight at the Abandoned Cove

The twilight breaks on weary rocks,
Where time has worn away the clocks.
An echo calls from deep within,
As secrets murmur with the din.

The cove awaits, with eyes so bright,
Embracing dusk's enchanting light.
Each wave retreats, a story brief,
A symphony of joy and grief.

The ships long gone, their sails now frayed,
In whispers soft, their debts are paid.
On gentle breezes, memories glide,
In every breath, the past resides.

Yet still the stars begin to burn,
As tides recede, for night's return.
In twilight's grasp, a secret spell,
Where time and tides forever dwell.

Relics of the Ocean Floor

Where whispers of the ocean dwell,
The relics weave their ancient spell.
A treasure trove of time and tide,
In secrets lost, where dreams abide.

The coral blooms like painted lace,
In colors that the sun can trace.
Each shell is carved with stories grand,
Of journeys taken, far-off lands.

As currents swirl, the past awakes,
In every crest, the heartache breaks.
The ghosts of sailors' lullabies,
In salt and sea, their memory lies.

From depths below, a message clear,
The ocean sings, we long to hear.
With every wave, a breath of fate,
The relics whisper, never late.

The Song of the Tides

The tides they rise, the tides they fall,
A symphony that calls us all.
In every crest, a rhythm found,
A dance of water, joy unbound.

The whispers swirl along the shore,
Each gentle wave, an ancient score.
With every roll, a story hums,
A world awakened, softly comes.

The moonbeam's touch, it guides the way,
Through shifting sands, where shadows play.
The ocean's voice, a lullaby,
That soothes the soul, and lifts the sky.

In perfect harmony, they weave,
A tapestry of dreams to leave.
The song of tides, forever wide,
In waves of wonder, we confide.

The Mermaid's Hidden Passage

In waters deep where secrets lie,
A mermaid sings with a curious sigh.
Her passage veiled by shimmering waves,
Guided by light through coral caves.

With flickering fins, she twirls and sways,
In twilight's glow, her beauty plays.
Adventure calls from depths unknown,
A realm where dreams and whispers groan.

Amongst the shells, her laughter weaves,
Echoing softly through seaweed leaves.
Each treasure found tells tales of old,
Of braver souls and hearts of gold.

A light that dances on ocean's crest,
In her hidden passage, find your quest.
For magic thrives in the deep blue sea,
Where the enchanting tides set spirits free.

So dive beneath the silver light,
Let the waves carry you to flight.
Follow her song, let your heart be brave,
And uncover the dreams that the sea gave.

Beneath the Brine and Time

Beneath the brine, where shadows glide,
The whispered tales of ages bide.
Each grain of sand a moment holds,
Of ancient mariners and stories told.

The sea, a tapestry of the past,
Holds memories wrapped in mysteries vast.
Where time flows like the rolling tide,
The spirits of sailors dance and glide.

Coral palaces, their colors bright,
Guard vibrant dreams from day to night.
Beneath the waves, in silence deep,
A world awakens from its sleep.

Echoing songs of the ocean's heart,
Every ripple a work of art.
Through shifting currents, secrets found,
In the quiet depths, wonder abounds.

So listen close and you'll hear the chime,
Of stories woven in brine and time.
For nature speaks in whispers clear,
To those who venture, hearts sincere.

Where Iron Meets the Siren's Song

Where iron meets the siren's song,
A clash of realms, both fierce and strong.
The lighthouses stand, their beams aglow,
Guarding the shores where sailors go.

With echoes deep, the oceans call,
A melody sweet that entraps us all.
The tides will rise, the storms will crest,
Yet still her song holds hearts at rest.

Amongst the rocks, the sirens dance,
In swirling waves, a spellbinding trance.
Their voices blend with the howling wind,
Weaving a charm that lures us in.

The ships may falter, the anchors sway,
But in the depths, dreams find their way.
For where the iron meets the sea,
The siren's song sings wild and free.

So heed the call, let the music rise,
As ocean waves caress the skies.
In harmony, find your way along,
And sail forever on the siren's song.

Shadows of Forgotten Sea Conch

In shadows cast by the ocean's hand,
Forgotten tales in the shifting sand.
A conch shell rests, a secret holds,
Of lost expanse and treasures bold.

With every whisper of the tide,
Memories linger, can't be denied.
The echoes call of what's left behind,
In twilight's hush, all truths unwind.

The moonlight dances on waves of blue,
Illuminating paths once walked by few.
In its embrace, the conch reveals,
A legacy that time conceals.

The sailors' laughter still fills the air,
Boundless adventures beyond compare.
As shadows play, a story unfolds,
In the heart of the ocean, the past beholds.

So listen well, for the sea will teach,
In the silence, wisdom's speech.
For shadows whisper, quiet yet strong,
The legacy of the ocean's song.

Whispers from the Coral Gate

Beneath the waves, where shadows twist,
A secret world that few have kissed.
Coral blooms sing in hues so bright,
Their whispers weave through the moonlight.

Stories old and treasures lost,
Each tide reveals what dreams embossed.
The sea an oracle, wise and deep,
In silence, all its secrets keep.

Upon the shore, the breezes dance,
Carrying tales of chance and romance.
With every ebb, a promise made,
In watery realms, the heart can't fade.

Crabs gather 'round, in soft twilight,
Listening close to the sea's delight.
With shells as drums, they tap in time,
To the rhythm of the ocean's rhyme.

From depths uncharted, come and see,
The coral gate calls out to thee.
In every whisper, a truth awaits,
Where dreams converge at the coral gates.

The Enchanted Portcullis

Guarded by shadows, the portcullis stands,
With ivy entwined in delicate bands.
A bridge to places unseen, yet near,
A passage forth, where none may fear.

The moonlight glints on rusted chains,
Awakening echoes of ancient reigns.
Glimmers of magic in the night,
Tales of wonder ready to ignite.

Whispers of fairies around the bend,
Calling for brave hearts to descend.
Beyond the gate, where dreams unite,
Lies a world painted in pure delight.

Eldritch symbols, carved with care,
Hold the secrets of magic rare.
Each word a spell, each sigh a song,
Inviting all to join where they belong.

With courage bold, approach the sound,
Where the heart's true desires are found.
The enchanted portcullis opens wide,
A gateway deep where dreams abide.

Tales from the Salt-Crusted Threshold

At the threshold where land meets sea,
Whispers of legends drift to me.
Salt-kissed breezes carry old lore,
Stories of shipwrecks and lovers' shore.

Once fierce storms raged, ships lost in waves,
But brave souls linger within the caves.
Their tales are woven with whispers low,
Of hidden treasures and love's sweet glow.

The threshold beckons with winds that sigh,
Promising journeys where fantasies lie.
Footprints etched in the weathered sand,
Map the adventures of a time so grand.

Gulls wheel overhead, their cries a song,
Calling the brave to where they belong.
With hearts ablaze and visions clear,
They step across, casting off fear.

Tales of yore, from salt-crusted rise,
Invite all dreamers with open eyes.
Find your path where the ocean swells,
At the threshold where the story dwells.

The Ocean's Timeworn Gatekeeper

Upon the shore, a figure stands,
The gatekeeper wise, with weathered hands.
His eyes reflect the ocean's depth,
Guarding secrets, the world has kept.

Years have passed by like the tide,
Yet in his gaze, memories abide.
With every wave that breaks on stone,
He hears the voices of those long gone.

His tales are spun from salt and foam,
Whispers of sailors who seek a home.
Each story borne on the crest of a wave,
Bringing life to those the sea could save.

In twilight's glow, he shares his grace,
Inviting wanderers to join the chase.
With a gentle nod, he keeps them near,
To safeguard dreams and quell their fear.

For time is but a fleeting friend,
And in each story, we find a blend,
Of past and present, forever stirred,
By the gatekeeper's magic, softly purred.

The Keeper of Ocean Secrets

In shimmering depths where shadows play,
A sentry guards the dreams that stray.
With whispered tales on currents gliding,
Her secrets held, in waves confiding.

Beneath the foam, where silence reigns,
Ancient songs weave through the grains.
The tides reveal what time forgot,
In every tide, a story caught.

Stars above like lanterns glow,
Guiding sailors to hidden flow.
Her breath, the breeze that lifts the sails,
In salty mist, adventure hails.

Where mermaids dance in moonlit beams,
And every shell conceals its dreams.
The Keeper smiles, her watchful gaze,
On whispered paths of ocean's maze.

With a heart attuned to every sound,
She knows the echoes that abound.
A guardian of the deep blue sea,
Her mysteries, forever free.

Fantasies Beneath the Waterline

Beneath the surface, dreams entwine,
In fragrant kelp, lost thoughts combine.
Fish weave tales through currents strong,
A ballet shared in ocean's song.

Coral castles, bright and grand,
With secret doors to fairyland.
The flicker of fins, a fleeting trace,
Hints of magic in this hidden space.

Bright jellyfish like lanterns float,
Guiding spirits, a mystical boat.
In the depths, time dances slow,
As forgotten hopes begin to grow.

The shadows of whales hum low and deep,
They carry dreams from fathoms steep.
In peace they glide, with wisdom vast,
Guardians of futures, echoes past.

Each ripple holds a story untold,
Treasures of the heart, brave and bold.
In the cool embrace of ocean's sway,
Fantasies call, we drift away.

Tethered to the Moonlit Waves

The moonlight casts a silver sheen,
On restless tides where dreams convene.
A tethered heart, in rhythm beats,
With pulsing waves, where passion meets.

Each swirl and crest, a dance of fate,
Invites the soul, it can't wait.
As night unfolds her darkened shroud,
The ocean hums, both fierce and proud.

With every splash, a wish ignites,
Floating lanterns in starry nights.
The whispers beckon, soft and sweet,
As echoes pulse beneath our feet.

In tidal dreams, we lose our way,
While shadows blend in a watery play.
A love that flows beyond the shore,
Yearns to be free, to crave for more.

So let the moonlight guide our course,
Through every wave, a gentle force.
In each embrace of night we find,
The tethered truth of heart and mind.

The Language of Forgotten Echoes

In caverns deep where silence dwells,
The echoes stir with secret spells.
Whispers of fish in currents glide,
A language lost, where dreams abide.

The sound of water sings so clear,
Of memories shared, of joy and fear.
Anselm's tune, with laughter twined,
The past and present well aligned.

Among the stones, resistance fades,
In ebb and flow, the melody wades.
Cascading voices, sweet and low,
Their symphony, a river's flow.

A flicker sharp in twilight's glow,
The secrets of the deep to show.
In harmony, they weave their tale,
Of shipwrecked dreams and gentle gale.

So lend your ear to these soft calls,
Beneath the waves, where mystery sprawls.
For in each ripple, life's song remains,
The language sung, through love and pains.

Mysteries Beneath the Surface

In depths elusive, secrets lay,
Whispers of old in waters sway.
Mirrored skies, reflections gleam,
Beneath the waves, a silent dream.

Ancient ships, their tales untold,
Treasures lost, enshrined in gold.
Echoes linger, soft yet clear,
Calling forth what we hold dear.

Creatures dance in shadows cast,
Time forgotten, shadows vast.
What lies beneath, a curious call,
To seek the truth, to rise and fall.

Mysterious depths, a beckoning hand,
Guiding us through this enchanting land.
A journey marked by hopes and fears,
The beauty lingers, though it disappears.

With every wave, a story spun,
Of worlds unseen, where dreams are won.
In depths we find the heart's delight,
In mysteries where shadows light.

The Slow Embrace of Sea Foam

Gentle waves, a soft caress,
Inviting calm, inviting rest.
The sea foam clings like whispered sighs,
A tender touch where silence lies.

With every tide, a lover's kiss,
The salty breeze, a moment's bliss.
Frothy curls in sunlit rays,
Hold memories of long-lost days.

The ocean's pulse, a steady beat,
Syncs with the heart, so bittersweet.
It draws us close, then sets us free,
To dance within its mystery.

Currents churn in a slow embrace,
Time drifts softly, a gentle trace.
In sea foam's grasp, we lose our cares,
In ocean's depth, our spirit flares.

A dance of light on the ocean's face,
Where love and longing find their place.
With open arms, the sea will greet,
Embracing souls in rhythmic beat.

Shadows of the Abyss

Into the dark where silence reigns,
Shadows flicker, the mind contains.
What lurks below, we cannot know,
In the deep, where dim lights glow.

Ancient beings, with eyes aglow,
Watch from depths where few dare go.
Legends whisper of timeless plight,
In shadows where the eerie light.

The pull of the void, a siren's song,
Calls to the brave, the weak, the strong.
When currents swirl, we all must choose,
To seek the dark or face the blues.

Secrets hidden in murky glades,
Lost amid the ancient shades.
But in the dark, truths often weave,
A tapestry of what we believe.

The abyss holds both fear and grace,
In its depths, we find our place.
To brave the shadows, we must descend,
And trust the journey 'til the end.

The Key to a Vanished Realm

In whispers soft, a key is found,
To realms where dreams and shadows bound.
Unlocking doors to unseen lands,
Where magic weaves with unseen hands.

Through twisted paths and ancient trees,
The air is laced with mysteries.
With every turn, a secret near,
The past ignites, the future clear.

In twilight's glow, the spirits rise,
To guide our hearts to paradise.
With courage firm and minds set free,
We step through realms of fantasy.

A journey marked by heart and soul,
With every moment, we become whole.
In endless night and shining dawn,
The key we hold, forever drawn.

To vanished realms, we now must go,
Where wonders bloom and shadows flow.
In every key, a story's thread,
Unlock the dreams we cling to, spread.

Crumbling Structures of a Lost Age

Ancient stones that softly weep,
Lost tales in shadows deep.
Faded glory, whispers sigh,
Echoes of a time gone by.

Mossy halls where secrets hide,
Dreams of kings who ruled with pride.
Windows cracked, a view of grey,
History's ghost begins to play.

Silent whispers fill the air,
Memories of those who dared.
Crumbling walls, a fractured past,
Time's relentless hand holds fast.

Cobwebs dance in faded light,
Phantoms weave the day's twilight.
Each lost brick a story told,
Fragments of a heart of gold.

Beneath the weight of weary years,
Structures sigh through hidden tears.
Yet in decay, there's life anew,
Crumbling age keeps dreaming true.

The Whispers of Distant Shores

Beneath the stars, the ocean calls,
Whispers dance through moonlit halls.
Far away the breezes sigh,
Secrets sail on ships gone by.

Waves embrace the sandy beach,
Stories linger, just out of reach.
Foamy tides and seagulls soar,
Echoes of what came before.

Shells conceal the tales of yore,
Lost loves dwell on every shore.
In the mist, shadows appear,
Ghostly laughter, drawing near.

Each grain of sand a tale to tell,
Of treasure found and broken spell.
Where the sea meets the twinkling night,
Fleeting dreams take flight in light.

The horizon beckons with a grin,
Endless journeys waiting to begin.
In every whisper, in every wave,
The heart of the ocean, wild and brave.

Navigating Through Bedrock Dreams

In the depths of night's embrace,
Whispers guide a hidden place.
Through the dark, a lantern gleams,
Navigating through bedrock dreams.

Footsteps falter, shadows play,
Mapping paths where lost hopes lay.
Beneath the earth, secrets lie,
Roots of ancient stories cry.

Mysterious echoes call my name,
Illuminated fears and flame.
Carved in stone, the past remains,
Promises whispered through the chains.

Yet in this cavern's silent beat,
Courage grows with every feat.
Through the maze of what has been,
Found within the heart, a kin.

With each step, the shadows part,
Guided by a steadfast heart.
Bedrock dreams, a timeless quest,
A journey towards the very best.

Threads of Time Bound in Seaweed

Twisted strands of kelp unwind,
Echoes of the sea entwined.
Each green thread a memory spun,
Threads of time, now come undone.

Sunken ships with tales to tell,
Beneath the waves, they weave and swell.
In the depths where light is rare,
Seaweed cradles whispered air.

Tides of fate pull us along,
In this dance, we find the strong.
Ancient mariners' dreams still soar,
Bound in seaweed, forevermore.

Laughter of the ocean's breeze,
Sings of lives lost in the seas.
As we drift, the past reveals,
The countless stories time conceals.

Through the depths, our hopes emerge,
Carried forth on water's verge.
Threads of time, as we endeavor,
Bound in seaweed, now and ever.

Secrets Beneath the Surface

In whispered waves, the secrets sleep,
Where shadows dance and silence creeps.
Beneath the foam, a world concealed,
With tales of woe, yet dreams revealed.

A treasure trove of thoughts unsaid,
Lost in the depths, where visions tread.
The moonlight glimmers, soft and pale,
As secrets weave their timeless tale.

The coral reefs, a vibrant throng,
Guard every hush, every song.
In hushed tones echoing in the deep,
Ancient wonders still to keep.

Through murky waters, heartbeats race,
In quest of truth, we find our place.
A voyage yearning, hearts entwined,
To find the secrets left behind.

A Lament for the Lost Tide

The tide retreats, with heavy sighs,
As dreams dissipate beneath grey skies.
Once vibrant shores now shimmer pale,
Echoes of laughter in the gale.

The sea once sang a lulling tune,
A dance of waves beneath the moon.
Now silence reigns where joy once flowed,
A haunting hush, a heavy load.

Each grain of sand recalls the light,
Of sun-kissed days and starlit nights.
But tides they turn, and seasons change,
The heart of the sea feels ever strange.

A memory lingers, bittersweet,
Of moments past and times complete.
Yet still we dream of shores we seek,
Though lost in time, we're never weak.

The Siren's Hidden Sanctuary

In hidden coves, where whispers blend,
The siren waits, her voice to send.
With shimmering scales and eyes of night,
She lures the lost with song and light.

Her sanctuary, a secret place,
With rippling waves, a soft embrace.
Where love and longing gently weave,
And hearts believe what hearts perceive.

The sailors' dreams drift on the breeze,
While time unravels with such ease.
In every note, a story spun,
Of hope and loss, of battles won.

Yet caveats echo through the song,
Of perilous paths where few belong.
For in her gaze, both sweet and wild,
Lies magic woven, undefiled.

Shadows of the Unseen Depths

Where shadows linger, depths conceal,
The whispered truths that few can feel.
In silent gulfs, the secrets nest,
In twilight's hush, they wait for rest.

The echoes call from ages past,
In briny waves, their stories cast.
Each ripple tells of long-lost dreams,
Of bitter tears and sunlit beams.

Among the rocks, the silence grows,
A tranquil peace where darkness flows.
Yet in the dark, a light might gleam,
As shadows dance in shadowed schemes.

For every heart that dares to dive,
Finds depths unknown, where spirits thrive.
A journey deep, away from lies,
In shadows' grasp, true wisdom lies.

The Key to Atlantis' Heart

In dreams of blue, where shadows play,
Lie secrets deep, in tides' ballet.
A city lost, with whispers strong,
The key awaits, where hearts belong.

Beneath the waves, the phantoms glide,
In coral halls, where spirits bide.
A map of stars, through ocean's tease,
Unlock the door, with gentle ease.

In currents swift, a melody hums,
The heartbeats echo, where silence comes.
Ancient stones, with stories old,
Will lead the way, to treasures bold.

With every breath, the sea enthralls,
Through hidden paths, our fate installs.
So venture forth, with courage bright,
For Atlantis' heart, calls through the night.

Lullabies of Woven Seaweed

In twilight's glow, the sea sings low,
With lullabies where dreams might flow.
Woven seaweed, soft and light,
Cradles the stars in the calm of night.

The ocean's breath, a gentle sway,
Wraps the weary, drift away.
Each whispering wave, a loving caress,
Brings solace deep, a sweet redress.

Tangled in dreams, the mermaids weep,
For lost sailors in waters deep.
Yet woven seaweed, strong and bright,
Guides them home through the starry night.

In moonlit dances, tides align,
With songs of comfort, pure divine.
So close your eyes, let currents weave,
Lullabies sung, in magic believe.

Portals of the Abyssal Realm

Where shadows dwell, and light is rare,
Portals whisper, through midnight air.
Beneath the crest of rolling foam,
A hidden realm, where secrets roam.

In depths untold, the ancients wait,
Guarding entrances, twisting fate.
With every wave, a story churns,
In abyssal halls, where wisdom burns.

Trilobites dance in starlit streams,
Awakening echoes of ancient dreams.
Dive deep below, let courage steer,
Through portals vast, a world endear.

Lost are the maps, but hearts can find,
The paths that echo the ocean's mind.
In darkest waters, light will bloom,
As portals open, dispelling gloom.

Guardians of the Tidal Threshold

Where the sea meets the restless shore,
Guardians stand, forevermore.
With eyes like storm clouds, fierce and wide,
They shield the realm, where spirits bide.

In tides that rise, and winds that shout,
They guard the dreams, and cast out doubt.
With kraken's arm, and mermaid's song,
They keep the peace, where we belong.

On moonlit nights, they dance and sway,
Protecting realms until break of day.
With woven shells and coral crown,
They stand as watchmen, never drown.

But should the storm rage, and tempests rear,
The guardians call, instilling fear.
Yet storms must pass, as all things do,
The tide recedes, and peace breaks through.

A Symphony of Submerged Twists

In the depths where shadows play,
Whispers of fish flit and sway,
Coral towers rise and bloom,
Hidden secrets fill the room.

A melody of tides that call,
Each wave a rise, each dip a fall,
Octopus dances, swift and sly,
Underneath the endless sky.

Listen close for tales untold,
Of treasures lost and legends bold,
Where moonlight weaves through ocean's lace,
And time surrenders, leaving space.

In currents swift, enchantments bind,
With every twist, horizons unwind,
A symphony of heartbeats play,
As sea and soul drift far away.

Awash in hues of deep cerulean,
The heart of water, a palladium,
In silence, wonder finds its voice,
In this submerged, majestic choice.

Mysterious Keys in Saltwater Dreams

In twilight's glow, the sea does sigh,
A treasure hidden, nigh the sky,
Each grain of sand, a story spun,
Of whispers lost, of battles won.

Keyholes glimmer on the shore,
Unlocking dreams of yesteryore,
Among the waves, they drift and gleam,
Shimmering bright in saltwater dreams.

Mermaids' laughter calls the night,
As lanterns flicker, pure delight,
Mysteries wrapped in a salty breeze,
Waiting for hearts to seize and please.

With every tide, the past will dance,
In moonlit waves, a fleeting chance,
To hold the keys that time forgets,
In ocean's heart, our fate begets.

So tread with care on this fine line,
Where dreams and reality intertwine,
Embrace the sea, let worries fade,
As keys of magic are gently laid.

Underneath Serenity Lies

Beneath the calm of azure skies,
In silent depths, serenity lies,
Where gentle currents softly flow,
And secrets hide in ebb and glow.

The ocean's breath, a tranquil tune,
Reflecting light of sun and moon,
A tapestry of dreams untold,
In shades of blue, a heart of gold.

But stir the depths, and you will find,
A wildness lurking, unconfined,
A tempest fierce, a clash of might,
That shrouds the day and stirs the night.

What once was peace can quickly shift,
A hint of danger, Nature's gift,
Yet through the storms, hope still survives,
For underneath, serenity thrives.

A balance born from chaos passed,
In every wave, a truth amassed,
For after rain, the sun will rise,
Beneath the calm, where wonder lies.

Dancers in the Currents

Under the spell of moonlit beams,
Life twirls and bends in sparkling dreams,
Scales of silver flash and gleam,
As waters sway with a gentle stream.

Fins like ribbons in the night,
Each dancer captures soft twilight,
Their bodies whirl in fluid grace,
In ocean's arms, a warm embrace.

The rhythm echoes, a song divine,
Hearts entwined with the ebbing line,
A ballet played on nature's stage,
Where every tide tells a new page.

With every splash, a story spins,
Of laughter shared, of loves, and sins,
Let go the fears, and join the flow,
As dancers in the currents glow.

So heed the call of waves and foam,
For here, my friend, you find your home,
In harmony with sea and sky,
Where all is free, and spirits fly.

Erosion's Embrace at the Water's Edge

Waves whisper secrets to the shore,
Softly they call, forevermore.
Sands shift under the moon's pale gaze,
Time erodes in a silvery haze.

Stones worn smooth by the ocean's kiss,
Echoes of history in tranquil bliss.
Footprints fade where the tide once flowed,
Leaving behind tales untold.

The horizon stretches, vast and wide,
Carrying dreams on the turning tide.
Nature's rhythm, a dance of grace,
Erosion's embrace, a tender trace.

Shells tell stories of ocean's deep,
In their silence, ancient secrets keep.
Beneath the surface, life swirls and twirls,
In a magical world where mystery unfurls.

Crests rise high, then gently fall,
An endless cycle, a beckoning call.
At water's edge, where dreams collide,
The soul finds solace in the ebbing tide.

Beneath the Sound of the Sea

In the depths where shadows play,
The ocean sings a lullaby sway.
With echoes of whispers, soft and low,
Secrets of fables in currents flow.

A chorus of creatures, both near and far,
Dancing in rhythms, like a twinkling star.
The tide weaves tales of joy and despair,
Beneath the sound, dreams linger in air.

Anemone blooms in hues so bright,
Underneath waves that shimmer with light.
Life and motion, a vibrant ballet,
Beneath the sound of the sea's soft play.

Listen closely, feel the embrace,
Of a watery world, a magical space.
For there lies wisdom in the ocean's heart,
A melody sweet, a living art.

With each cresting wave, stories unfold,
Tales of the brave, the timid, the bold.
In the depths, where life's symphony sways,
Beneath the sound, the sea always stays.

The Chronicles of Coral Guardians

In the heart of the reef, a guardian stands,
Colorful dreams shaped by nature's hands.
Coral unfolds in vibrant delight,
A fortress of life in the perpetual light.

Tiny fish dart through the intricate maze,
In the guardians' watch, a mystical gaze.
Each branch and crevice a home, a nest,
In the ocean's embrace, where life finds rest.

Tides ebb and flow, as time marches on,
Yet steadfast remain the coral and dawn.
Whispers of wisdom in currents so clear,
Guardians of peace amid beauty and fear.

Seashells listen to tales of old,
Legends of guardians, so brave and bold.
In every hue, a story is spun,
Of the chronicles sung beneath the sun.

Yet storms may come and threaten their reign,
But the guardians stand, enduring the pain.
For in each trial, life's strength grows strong,
The chronicles echo in nature's song.

Dunes of Time and Relics

Whispers of sand in a melodic drift,
Carry the stories of time's gentle lift.
Dunes roll like waves under starlit skies,
A haven for dreams where the past never dies.

Forgotten relics sleep beneath the sand,
Echoes of fortune from a long-lost land.
Bones of ships that dared to roam,
Now resting here, far from home.

The winds caress with a soft, sweet sigh,
Guiding the grains as they slip and fly.
Each shift of the dune, a chapter erased,
In the book of the world, where time is traced.

Footprints wander, then fade away,
Leaving behind what the wind may sway.
In the silence of dusk, where the sun sets slow,
Dunes of time hum the tales they know.

As shadows stretch long, and twilight falls,
The horizon blushes as the night calls.
In soft whispers, the sandbars pine,
For the relics of heart woven through time.

Embracing the Echoes of Silence

In shadows deep, where whispers play,
The echoes dance in twilight gray.
Time holds its breath, the world stands still,
In silence, dreams begin to thrill.

A gentle heart, like breezes sigh,
Listens close as memories fly.
Within the hush, the truth unfolds,
In softened tones, the heart consoles.

Ghosts of yore in silence weave,
Tales of joy, of hurt, we grieve.
Each lingering sound, a guiding star,
Reminds us just how near, how far.

We walk the paths where silence breathes,
In every shadow, the spirit seethes.
Embrace the quiet, let it speak,
For in stillness, we grow unique.

In echoes found, we find our place,
A serenade of time and space.
So hush your doubts, let silence reign,
For here lies peace from joy and pain.

Secrets Under the Sailor's Heart

Beneath the stars, where oceans weep,
A sailor's heart holds secrets deep.
With every wave that whispers low,
A tale of love, a hidden glow.

The compass spins with dreams untold,
Guided by winds both fierce and bold.
In every storm that tests his might,
Resides a wish to find the light.

Anchored firm in troubled seas,
He searches for his heart's sweet ease.
In every port, a gaze turned back,
Yearning for shores once left untracked.

Yet in the depths, where shadows dwell,
The secrets land, a tranquil swell.
For hidden treasures lie beneath,
The sailor's heart, the vast sea's wreath.

In quiet moments, stories flare,
Each tide reveals a love laid bare.
So when the stars above ignite,
Listen close, feel the sailor's plight.

Tides Turning Around Withered Edges

The tides they turn, with gentle grace,
Caressing shores that time can't erase.
Withered edges tell tales of old,
Of hearts once warm, now bitter cold.

As waves embrace the crumbling land,
They whisper softly, hand in hand.
Each ebb and flow, a pulse divine,
Of love lost deep, like ancient wine.

Beneath the surface, life still stirs,
While echoes linger, time confirms.
In silken strands of ocean's weave,
We find the strength to love, believe.

The sun dips low, as shadows play,
And memories etched in sands decay.
Yet through the change, hope remains bright,
A beacon shining through the night.

So let the tides, with soft caress,
Heal all the wounds, the hurt, the stress.
For every edge that's worn and bare,
Is wrapped in dreams, in salt and air.

The Latch of Forgotten Stories

In secret nooks where memories hide,
Whispers linger, never died.
A latch once turned, now rusted slow,
Opens to worlds we yearn to know.

Forgotten tales in dusty books,
Invite us gently with stolen looks.
In corners dark, where shadows creep,
The echoes of old secrets seep.

Each page a portal, each word a key,
Unlocking doors to what used to be.
In every line, a truth unfolds,
The hearts of many, their hope enfolds.

As twilight draws the curtain low,
We find the light through the ebb and flow.
Nostalgia sings in sweet refrain,
In whispered verses, joy and pain.

So linger here, let stories rest,
For in the past, they've been blessed.
Embrace the magic, let it soar,
For every tale opens a door.

Echoing Laughter Beneath the Surface

In the glimmering brook, laughter cries,
Rippling dreams beneath the skies.
Whispers of joy in a shimmering dance,
Where sunlight sparkles, and shadows prance.

Bubbles rise forth, secrets they keep,
Echoing laughter from the depths so deep.
With every flicker, a tale unfolds,
Of brave little fish and wonders untold.

Stones lie still, with stories to share,
Of daring little adventures that dare.
A current of whispers, a splash so bright,
As moonbeams sprinkle the soft twilight.

Beneath the surface, where silence sings,
A treasure of memories the water brings.
Joyful mirth where the currents spin,
In the heart of the stream, we all begin.

A dance with the waves, a fluttering play,
Where the laughter lingers and wishes stay.
In the depths of the world, the echoes ring,
Beneath the surface, our souls take wing.

Locks of Driftwood and Dreamscapes

Twists of driftwood, worn and wise,
Carved by the tides, kissed by the skies.
Each grain a story, each curve a dream,
Floating on currents, like whispers of steam.

In the shadows danced, the moonlight glows,
Where time meanders and magic flows.
Locks of the water, wild and free,
Guarding the secrets of you and me.

In slumbering groves where the dreamers sigh,
Nature's embrace under the vast night sky.
Each moment cherished, each heartbeat felt,
In a world of wonder, where magic is dealt.

A symphony plays on a breeze of sound,
Driftwood and dreams where enchantments abound.
Weave me a tale of adventure's flight,
In a tapestry woven of starlit night.

Through the whispers of leaves, a lilt of song,
With locks of driftwood, we all belong.
In this realm, our imaginations soar,
Where dreams unfurl on the ocean's floor.

Secrets Wrapped in Tidal Veils

Under the moonlight, soft and clear,
Secrets are brought forth, voices to hear.
Wrapped in the waves, like treasures rare,
The tides reveal wonders, whispered with care.

Shells cradle echoes from ages long past,
Stories of sailors and storms fierce and vast.
Each layered whisper, a tale of the sea,
In the embrace of the waves, wild and free.

Tidal veils shimmering in the night,
Holding their secrets with all of their might.
The ocean's true heart, a canvas of dreams,
Painting our thoughts in its endless streams.

Hidden below, where the mysteries glide,
Ancient enchantments in glistening tide.
With every ebb, a promise unfolds,
Of magic and wonder yet to be told.

In the depths of the waters, a floating dance,
Secrets await in a mystical trance.
Wrapped in the tide, our souls intertwine,
Whispers of the sea, forever divine.

Riddles in the Clam Shell Door

Upon the shore, where the waves collide,
Clam shell doors beckon with secrets inside.
Riddles that sparkle like stars in the night,
Awaiting the brave who seek out the light.

With a gentle whisper, it opens anew,
Unveiling the treasures, the old and the true.
A labyrinth of dreams in a shell's tender curve,
Where the heart of the ocean begins to serve.

Each hidden pearl holds a story to tell,
Of enchantments lost in a silken shell.
The riddles they guard, like riddles of fate,
Unlock the adventure, it's never too late.

Turn the keys of wisdom with laughter and cheer,
Discover the magic that lingers near.
For deep in the shell lies a world unexplored,
A wondrous escape through the clam shell door.

So listen closely to the ocean's soft tune,
Secrets await where the tide meets the moon.
With every riddle and laugh we implore,
The joy of the journey forever in store.

Whispers of Salt and Rust

Upon the shore where shadows play,
The whispers rise with dawn's soft gleam.
Salt-kissed winds sing tales of sway,
Of ships that danced upon a dream.

Beneath the stars, the past awakes,
Rusty anchors tell of time.
Each grain of sand, the ocean makes,
A tapestry, both rich and prime.

Tales of sailors lost at sea,
Adrift in storms that roar and cry.
Yet in their hearts, forever free,
They sail where timeless spirits fly.

With every wave, a secret spills,
Of haunted harbors, long since cast.
Echoes linger, as night instills,
A magic tethered to the past.

So listen close, the sea will share,
The stories woven in the air.
Whispers of salt, in rust we trust,
In every heart, a trace of dust.

The Forgotten Melody of Coral

In depths where light begins to fade,
The coral sings in softest hum.
A melody, both bright and frayed,
Of lovers lost, and waters numb.

Eldest seashells hold the tune,
Of ocean's love, both fierce and pure.
Their echoes dance 'neath silver moon,
In every heart, a lullaby's lure.

Once vibrant reefs, now painted gray,
Whisper secrets touched by time.
Yet still the currents weave and sway,
In perfect rhythm, just sublime.

And when the tide begins to rise,
The whispers call from deep below.
A haunting breeze, a soft reprise,
Of tales that ebb like wind and flow.

Remember well the coral's song,
For in its notes, we all belong.

Beneath the Waves of Memory

In twilight's grasp, the waters gleam,
Beneath the waves, the shadows shift.
Memory whispers, like a dream,
Of hidden treasures, lost but drift.

The ocean's depth, a canvas wide,
Painted with stories, rich and rare.
Each ripple yearns to be a guide,
To moments caught in salty air.

Ghostly ships and phantoms glide,
Through realms of blue, both vast and deep.
In silence, they begin to bide,
The secrets held, the oceans keep.

When storms arrive, the past returns,
Each wave a voice, a tale retold.
In heartbeats close, the spirit yearns,
For echoes buried in the cold.

So dive beneath the cresting foam,
Embrace the weight of olden days.
For in those depths, we find a home,
Where time dissolves in gentle ways.

Echoes of Enchantment in Driftwood

Among the trees where whispers roam,
Driftwood lies in sunlit grace.
Each knot and gnarled twist, a home,
For stories time cannot replace.

The forest hums a tender tune,
As shadows weave through roots and bark.
In twilight's gleam, beneath the moon,
Echoes of magic pierce the dark.

Tales of wanderers lost in haze,
Their laughter caught in tangled vines.
In every splinter, light displays,
A shimmering thread of ancient signs.

The dance of seasons, ebb and flow,
Carves wisdom in the wood's embrace.
Through whispered tales, the spirits grow,
Enchanted dreams, we all must trace.

So linger here, 'neath branches wide,
Feel the pulse that weaves each hour.
In driftwood's heart, our souls collide,
Where nature breathes her timeless power.

Fantastic Beasts of the Deep

In the shadows, creatures glide,
Mysteries of the ocean wide.
With scales that shimmer, dark and bright,
They dance beneath the silver light.

A kraken's whisper, soft and low,
In currents deep where wonders flow.
The sirens call with haunting song,
Enticing sailors to drift along.

Coral castles, homes of grace,
Where mermaids dwell in a sacred place.
Octopus dreams unfold like art,
Each tentacle a beating heart.

From primordial depths, they rise anew,
Guardians of secrets, old and true.
In the deep, a world entwined,
With fables carved, in silence lined.

So dive into the azure deep,
Where ancient legends softly sleep.
In the realms where time does cease,
The magic flows like waves of peace.

The Pulse of an Ocean Heart

Beneath the waves, the world awakes,
With every tide, a heartbeat shakes.
A symphony of whispers clear,
The ocean's pulse, so close, so near.

Echoes of giants, long since gone,
Shaping the depths from dusk till dawn.
A blue whale's song, a lullaby,
A timeless tale that soars the sky.

In the froth of surf, a fleeting dance,
Crabs scuttle quick, in a hurried trance.
The shimmer of fish, a fleeting glance,
Life teems below, in a wondrous expanse.

Soft shadows loom where darkness dwells,
In caverns deep with ancient spells.
The ocean heart beats wild and free,
An endless song beneath the sea.

Listen closely, hear its call,
In every rise, in every fall.
The pulse of life, a dance divine,
In ocean's arms, our fate entwined.

Fables Lurking in Marine Depths

In murky depths where shadows creep,
Lurk fables old, secrets to keep.
Tales of treasure, lost and found,
Echo in whispers, a haunting sound.

Glimmers of gold along the floor,
Awake the dreams of sailors' lore.
A compass lost, the map betrayed,
In depths where legends softly fade.

The narwhal sings of ancient rights,
In icy realms where magic ignites.
A shipwrecked heart, a ghostly tear,
In the saline mist, a story near.

The dolphin dances, wisdom refined,
In caverns where colors intertwine.
Each ripple stirs a tale untold,
Of bravery, love, and hearts so bold.

So heed the waves, their whispers clear,
For fables linger, ever near.
In the depths of blue, the lore ignites,
A tapestry woven in starry nights.

The Enigma of Barnacle Dreams

Upon the rocks where barnacles cling,
Lie dreams adrift, soft as a spring.
In cracks and crevices, stories nest,
Of tides that whisper, and hearts at rest.

A crab scuttles, a watchful gaze,
As currents shift in a salty haze.
Beneath each shell, a life concealed,
In secrets of stone, the past revealed.

The moon bewitches, pulling low,
While barnacles bask in a gentle glow.
Their tales entwined with ocean's breath,
In fleeting moments, surrounded by depth.

Seashells echo the dreams of yore,
Of sea sprites dancing on the shore.
In every crack, an echo beams,
Of lost desires and barnacle dreams.

So sit awhile, lose track of time,
Where barnacles harbor their tales sublime.
In the dance of salt, coastlines gleam,
Awash in the rhythm of ocean dreams.

The Doorway to Forgotten Dreams

In shadows deep where whispers lie,
A doorway waits, beneath the sky.
With threads of hope and ancient seam,
It beckons forth forgotten dream.

Through cobwebbed halls and echoes clear,
The laughter of the past draws near.
With every step, a dawning light,
Unveils the secrets held so tight.

Beneath the arch of time's embrace,
Each fleeting thought a cherished trace.
In murmur soft, the spirits sing,
Of lost tomorrows, years shall bring.

To those who dare to seek their fate,
A world beyond the ordinary gate.
With hearts ablaze and souls set free,
They find the path to memory.

The final key, a tender tear,
Unlocks the door, and hope draws near.
In every heartbeat, worlds collide,
Where dreams reside, and fears subside.

Coral Castles and Rusty Locks

By moonlit tide, the castles gleam,
Of coral bright, a lost heart's dream.
With rusty locks, they stand and sway,
Guarding the treasures of the bay.

The ocean's breath, a siren's song,
Where wayward souls have wandered long.
Amidst the waves, tales come alive,
In the depths, forgotten dreams thrive.

Each stone a whisper, each shell a voice,
In the depths, where all hearts rejoice.
In swirling sand, and gleaming light,
Lie secrets veiled from mortal sight.

With gentle hands, the sea draws near,
To kiss the shores, to calm all fear.
Rusty locks shall crumble down,
As dawn unfolds her golden crown.

Coral castles, timeless fate,
Unlock the dreams that lie in wait.
With open hearts, in waves we trust,
In the salt and spray, our spirits rust.

When Sheltered Waves Remember

Beneath the tide, where shadows play,
The sheltered waves hold thoughts at bay.
In gentle curls, and foam embraced,
They weave the memories, interlaced.

When silence dwells, the sea recalls,
The laughter lost and long-ago calls.
As time unwinds, so tenderly,
Each wave returns a memory.

With whispered tales of sailors bold,
And secrets deep, that fate has told.
In every crest, a story swells,
Of love, of loss, the heart compels.

The dance of tides, a rhythmic song,
Where dreams emerge and souls belong.
With open arms, the sea embraces,
The fleeting moments, time erases.

When sheltered waves remember well,
They break the silence, cast a spell.
In every drop, a world unseen,
Awakens hope, soft and serene.

Locks of Seaweed and Dreams

In hidden groves where currents twine,
The locks of seaweed twist and shine.
With dreams entwined in nature's art,
They cradle wishes in their heart.

Each strand a tale, a fable spun,
Beneath the waves where life has run.
With ocean's breath, they softly weave,
A tapestry of those who believe.

In salty air, where whispers dwell,
The echoes of a distant bell.
The call of tides, of hope's refrain,
Will guide the lost to find again.

With every ebb, and every flow,
The locks of seaweed gently grow.
Embracing dreams in shadows cast,
A promise of love, forever fast.

Each heartbeat dances in the deep,
Where secrets linger, and dreams can leap.
In locks of seaweed, tales are spun,
Of all that is, and all that's begun.

The Precarious Balance of Sleep

In twilight's hush, the dreams take flight,
Whispers weave through the silent night.
Restless minds, they dance and swoon,
While shadows play beneath the moon.

Soft murmurs of a gentle breeze,
Crooning tales from ancient trees.
Yet fear resides in slumber's hold,
A fragile balance, brave yet bold.

In twilight's clutch, the hours wane,
As sleep's sweet potion heals the pain.
But time, elusive, drifts away,
Haunting dreams that dare to stay.

With twinkling stars, the dreams collide,
Where secrets in the silence hide.
A thread unwinds, the dawn breaks clear,
Yet still we linger, lost in fear.

The fragile dance of night and morn,
In shadows deep, new dreams are born.
So hold your breath as you descend,
For every night must find its end.

Ancient Wood and Water Stories

In the heart of the forest where shadows play,
Ancient trees whisper secrets of day.
Beneath their boughs, the stories weave,
With every leaf, a tale to believe.

The rivers babble in melodic tongue,
Carrying echoes of songs long sung.
Cradled in currents, old spirits flow,
In every ripple, a memory glows.

Moss-clad giants with wisdom profound,
Guard the forgotten, the lost, and the found.
With roots like fingers, they grasp the ground,
In their shelter, enchantment is found.

Moonlit glades hold the breath of the night,
Where shadows stretch in the silver light.
The air is thick with the essence of lore,
Inviting the curious, to seek and explore.

So wander deep, where the wild things roam,
Ancient wood and water call you home.
For within their embrace, the stories flow,
A timeless journey, where dreams may grow.

The Veins Beneath the Surface

Beneath the skin, a world unseen,
Veins pulse with tales, both light and keen.
Whispers travel through darkened trails,
Carrying truth where silence prevails.

Colors bleed in forgotten hues,
Mapping journeys in hearts that choose.
Each heartbeat drums an echoing song,
A dance of life, both weak and strong.

Sculpted by time and tender care,
Threads of struggle weave through the air.
In the depth where secrets lie,
Vulnerable dreams dare to fly.

Yet shadows lurk, a haunting glance,
In the dance of fate, we take our chance.
Through the lattice of nerve and bone,
We seek connection, never alone.

So listen close to the whispers deep,
The veins beneath, their secrets keep.
For in the silence, stories arise,
A tapestry spun, beneath our skies.

Unlocking Limericks in the Darkness

In the quiet night, a riddle stirs,
A playful dance of words occurs.
With laughter's grace,
They find their place,
In moonlit corners where magic blurs.

The stanzas twist in gleeful jest,
Unlocking laughter, a joyful quest.
A play on the tongue,
Where dreams are flung,
In whimsical verses, we find our rest.

With each slight turn, a story spins,
Of unlikely heroes and cheeky wins.
Words like confetti,
A dance so ready,
To reveal what the dark truly brings.

In shadows, the rhythm begins to swell,
As tales entwine and secrets rebel.
A limerick's flight,
Through the still of the night,
Brings forth a laughter, a magic spell.

So gather 'round as the verses glow,
In the darkness, let reveries flow.
With a wink and a grin,
Let the fun begin,
Unlocking the joy in the limerick's show.

Rusty Locks and Ocean Tides

In a tower old, where shadows creep,
Rusty locks guard secrets deep.
The ocean whispers, waves will sigh,
Against the shores where memories lie.

Crimson skies above the sea,
Tales of love and mystery.
Each tide that rolls, brings stories old,
Of dreams once bright, now faded gold.

Beneath the stars that shimmer bright,
The sea weaves spells, both dark and light.
With every wave, a song to share,
Of hidden realms and hearts laid bare.

Rusty locks, a guardian still,
Hold the magic of the sea's will.
In whispered winds, the secrets glide,
Where the past and present collide.

So listen close, let your heart sail,
On ocean tides that tell the tale.
With each new dawn, take flight and dream,
In the embrace of the silky stream.

Secrets of the Worn Daedalus

In halls of stone, where echoes dwell,
The worn Daedalus spins his spell.
With whispers low and shadows cast,
Heals the wounds of a troubled past.

In labyrinths of fate entwined,
Secrets wait for hearts to find.
Step by step, the truth reveals,
A world of wonder, spun from wheels.

With every thread, a story spun,
Of battles lost and victories won.
In whispers soft, the legends call,
For those who dare to risk their all.

The fae will dance in twilight's glow,
Through corridors where time moves slow.
Each turn will guide the brave and bold,
To treasures hidden, dreams foretold.

Secrets linger, fate will bind,
The weary hearts, the lost, the blind.
In Daedalus's wise embrace,
Find the magic, find your place.

When the Sea Whispers Secrets

When the sea whispers secrets low,
Beneath the moon's soft silver glow.
Tales of ships in tempest tossed,
Of love once found and lovers lost.

Upon the shore, the sands reveal,
Echoes of a past, so surreal.
In waves that crash with thunderous might,
Lies the heart's longing, pure delight.

With time, the waters weave and spin,
Forging dreams from deep within.
Listen closely, the tide will sing,
Of the joy and pain that memories bring.

The gulls will cry, the stars will gleam,
As twilight hugs the sea's deep dream.
Secrets soar on the ocean's breath,
In every rise, a dance with death.

So heed the call of the gentle waves,
For in their swell, the heart enslaves.
As long as the tide and moon collide,
The sea will whisper, hearts will bide.

Echoes in the Rusted Depths

In depths where shadows twist and sway,
Echoes linger, lost in gray.
Rusty chains and vessels frayed,
Hold true whispers, time delayed.

The sailors' songs, now faint and dim,
Dance like phantoms, dark and grim.
Through wrecks of time, their tales persist,
In silent depths, they still exist.

Each ripple tells of salty tears,
Of hopes and dreams that lost their years.
Through corridors of sunken halls,
The memory of laughter calls.

In every fracture, every bruise,
The ocean holds its ancient muse.
With whispered words of love and loss,
The depths yield treasures, yet at cost.

So dive into this realm profound,
Where rusted echoes can be found.
Listen close, as stories weave,
In the heart of the sea, dare to believe.

Currents of an Ancient Tale

In shadows deep, the currents sway,
A tale unfurls, both night and day.
Whispers of yore in the moon's soft light,
Guide lost souls through the velvet night.

Time entangles, threads of fate,
Echoes linger, they wait and wait.
Each wave a secret, each turn a song,
In the depths, where we all belong.

Ancestors speak in the rippling sea,
Their voices weave in harmonious glee.
Legends rise with the tide's steady flow,
Carrying tales of long ago.

Beneath the surface, a world awaits,
A kingdom hidden behind fate's gates.
With courage as sail, we venture forth,
To find our purpose, our truest worth.

The current swirls, mysteries unfold,
An ancient tale, forever told.
Embrace the depths, forsake the shore,
For within the tale, we find our core.

Whispering Waves and Timeless Riddles

Whispering waves, a melodic cry,
Beneath the stars, where secrets lie.
Riddles echo, soft as the breeze,
In twilight's embrace, the heart finds ease.

Ripples dance with stories anew,
Each tide reveals what's hidden from view.
With every ebb, the past returns,
Flames of wisdom within us burns.

In the silence, a spell is cast,
Time's gentle hand, a tender grasp.
Treasures buried beneath the foam,
In whispers, the waves beckon us home.

Questions linger, we seek the light,
Lost in shadows, we wander, we write.
The ocean breathes, its timeless lore,
Guiding our spirits to distant shores.

As night unfurls its velvet cloak,
In the deepest bosom, a truth awoke.
Timeless riddles sung by the sea,
Whispering tales of what's yet to be.

The Veil Between Worlds

The veil between worlds, delicate, thin,
A glimmering whisper—a sacred hymn.
At dusk, it shimmers, blurs the line,
Where shadows linger, and stars align.

In twilight's grasp, the portals gleam,
Echoes of magic in a fleeting dream.
A dance of spirits, both near and far,
In the silence, they sing—a guiding star.

Softly they call, on the breath of night,
Stories entwined in the lunar light.
To journey beyond, with hearts aglow,
We step through the veil, where few dare to go.

In realms unknown, where the wild things roam,
We find lost whispers, we find our home.
With each gentle step, the past we trace,
In the veil's embrace, we find our place.

So hold to the dreams, let them unfurl,
For beyond the veil lies a wondrous world.
With hearts entwined, we bridge the divide,
In the dance of life, forever we ride.

Silhouettes in Brine and Stone

Silhouettes rise in the brine and stone,
Figures of memory, never alone.
Beneath the waves, where whispers blend,
The stories linger, and time transcends.

In ocean's grasp, the shadows sway,
Ancient spirits dance in their play.
Ethereal echoes, ageless and wise,
Navigating depths where the lost arise.

Each grain of sand, a tale to tell,
Of ships that ventured, of dreams that fell.
In every ripple, a heartbeat's trace,
Silhouettes linger in boundless space.

Embracing the night with a glimmering sigh,
We walk through the memories, never to die.
The tide reveals what the heart knows best,
In brine and stone, our souls find rest.

So let us wander, where shadows roam,
In the depths of the sea, we find our home.
With silhouettes dancing, our spirits soar,
In brine and stone, forevermore.

9 781805 628071